INTERNET AS AN OPPO OF WORKING LEGITIMA.LLI FROM INDIVIDUAL HOMES

A Broad Research Book towards online resources and investment Ideas to passive incomes for 2020 and years to come!

Forecast your success!

Written by:

Joe Cole

All Right Reserved To The Author.

Table of Contents:

1

Guideline on how to read this well researched Book:

It requires fundamental facilities such as infrastructure, investments & knowledgeable mindset:

Know your Market/Niche:

Have a plan towards your goal:

Guide against being defrauded online by scams:

Work Towards your goal:

HOW TO EARN MONEY LEGITIMATELY ONLINE

Being a computer literate i.e. Data entry job, Ability to do micro task, Typing jobs and much more:

Customer's services:

Generating income on fiverr:

Digital marketing skills:

Website design:

Building of sales funnels:

Content creators:

Graphic designs:

COPYRIGHT, LEGAL NOTICE & DISCLAIMER

[MY LEGAL ADVISER/ LAWYER DOES NOT ALLOW ME TO PUBLISH MY BOOKS WITHOUT LEGAL BACKINGS]

- Trademark, service & Everything about this Book belong to the owner and duplicated copy will not be accepted from anyone
- The author of this Book does not belong to any legal team he is a researcher and provide information that are genuine to the public.
- The methodology used in this Book can be used by anyone and would be of help to the public generally

Continuation of reading this Book is complying and understanding the above information listed below is in accordance to the legal tender of this Book.

INTRODUCTION

I must say a hearty thanks to you for purchasing this Valuable Book. I can say it with confidence you will get value from this Book that will change your life for good. Please anything you read in this Book take action on it for you to get a faster result, procrastination is the thief of time Because tomorrow never comes.

I can assure you that this Book will go a long way in influencing your life towards acquiring digital skills that will put food on your table anytime, any day and money will never be your problem again.

To be realistic it is very complicated to find a Marketing Business Book that is very Broad and very helpful lately.

This Book is well researched and will go a long way in anyone's life by taking action on the information provided in this Book.

This Book is all about doing little things that can guarantee passive incomes daily to the reader for the rest of his or her life. Me as a writer of this Book I started my Business with very little capital but with the help of daily new skills and Technology I can Boldly say it anytime any day that my Business is now globally standard, It does not happen overnight it is all about sacrifices and year of consistency that give me my desired dream Business. You can also do better by not procrastinating but by taking necessary actions towards it and self development is also very important.

This Book is all about Internet as a means of working legitimately from your homes

Internet is now the easiest way to make a good money now without going into cybercrime, fraudster, stealing of assets and much more. Some people see it as a means of making fast money by stealing of others people vital information, and deceiving people to invest their money on things that are not genuine then after payment of such money are made the investor will not be able to reach them again. It is very annoying and frustrating for someone to lose his or her hard work earnings to a fraudster online.

Before I proceed I will quickly define the term < INTERNET>

The Term Internet is a worldwide/global web of computers connected together with ease. It also helps people to share information between themselves without any stress and make life easier to live. Internet is a means of Building a legitimate passive income not a means of defrauding people i.e. through acquiring the necessary skills that will enable you to make a good living.

One of the Example is <writing>
Writers make a lot of money today because of the skills they have to educate people about the latest trends such as news publishing, publishing of magazines and also writing a manual and publishing it on Amazon and many other sites for readers to read and be educated about what is new in the society.

This little skill having been bringing Millions of Dollars to good writers yearly which I urge you to do the same by acquiring the skill rather than going into cyber crimes.

Guideline on how to read this well researched Book:

It requires fundamental facilities such as infrastructure, investments & knowledgeable mindset

Please note: When you start reading this Book from your end get the necessary equipment that will make you start acting on the new skills that this Book is all about. I would urge you to follow the steps listed below for you to get the Best out of this Book.

- Get a good computer be it a laptop or desktop, have a note, good internet & pen for you to write some vital information down and also use the computer to explore more about the new knowledge you come across.
- Do not get distracted when you start reading this book stay away from any means of distraction that will deprive you from concentrating while reading this Book. If you come across a vital information please stop reading and write it down in your Book for

further research that is the reason you have the Book and pen with you

- Get a bottle of water to prevent you from being thirsty to keep you hydrated and focus
- Have a daily plans for new skills you come across when reading this Book for you to get results faster because it is hallucination if you do not implement what you learn from this Book.

More so it is not about how many chapters of this book you have read, the important thing is taking action by implementing the new skills that is the only way you can get results faster and achieved a common goal.

Now we will be discussing about Infrastructure, investment & knowledgeable mindset to Earn money online.

They are as follows.

- A good computer & smartphone
- good internet connection with a good wifi router
- Conducive environment provided with Air condition, chair and a clean table to work.
- Ability to browse on internet & use of email as a means of communication to people.
- Ability to use the search engine to achieve a common goal called Google
- A good communication skill is required for business purpose.
- Ability to use the Microsoft Excel, Power point, Ms word & Corel draw for graphic designs
- Having International Bank account, credit & Debit card
- Ability type very well without an error is very important

- Ability to communicate fluently in English Language
- Ability to use the operating system, updating of system, Antivirus and much more.
- Ability to use the scanner and print out documents from the system.
- Ability to buy and sell goods online
- Digital marketing
- Good customers relationship

Know your Market/Niche

One of the key factors in any Business is to Know where your services are needed and positioning yourself as the grand commander in that Niche is very important. Because According to research 90% of Business will fail it is only 10% that will be successful and we need to be very careful not to lose our hard work earnings to a market that will not give us good return in the investment we made.

You need to be extraordinary careful in Business don't just say

- I want to invest in clothing Business
- I want to invest in Beauty/cosmetics
- I want to have a Business centre
- I want to have a gym centre
- I want to go into importation Business
- I want to have a school
- I want to be a consultant
- I want to invest in Travelling & Tourism.

You need to have a good plan and make a good research before you venture into any Businesses.

It is a good idea to say you want to do the Business listed Below, Besides, a lot of people are doing the exact same Business and they are successful in it and bring them millions & Billions so far.

My point here is that if you want to standout in a Business or a Niche you don't have to be doing what others have done. You need to be unique and creative enough for you to excel in the Business.

You need to make a proper research & take your time before you decide on the type of Business you intend to do.

I will educate you with a business idea but before we proceed with that we have to look into some issues first.

Your way of reasoning must be different from your competitors in the market so that you will not make the same mistakes others have made that kill their Business in the past i.e. Mistakes increases your experience and way of reasoning, Experience decreases your mistakes in anything you are doing, If you learn from your initial mistakes people will learn about your succ ess That is the fact .

The most important Business insight I will give you is this. Do not try to start a Business and then start looking for prospect to come and buy... Be a listener to the people yearnings once you discover people want venture into the Business and position yourself properly.

They will be the one rushing your products and you will make more money being a listener than investing without listening to the wants of the people.

The mistake most entrepreneurs make when they intend to start up a Business, this is the way they reason. They purchase the product and they start looking for

prospects to buy the product.
This is very wrong
The Best thing to do is research before venturing into any Business.
The explanation below is to let you know how most entrepreneurs think. That is why my approach to Business is different. I go into business after having seen a starving crowd that are ready to buy. You should cultivate that same habit to reduce your risk and make more money in your Business.

Have a plan towards your goal

The Term Plan is very important i.e. planning is the act, process of forecasting about an activities/ task to achieve a greater goal. It is the act of describing how the future will look like, and the 4 key elements of planning must be considered while

planning to move from a current
position to a desired position.

THE 4 KEY ELEMENTS OF PLANNING ARE AS FOLLOWS

OBJECTIVE
ACTION
IMPLEMENTATION

EXPLANATION OF THE 4 KEY ELEMENTS OF PLANNING ARE AS FOLLOWS

- OBJECTIVE: Is the no 1 key element of planning. It is one aim towards achieving a desired result or a common goal.
- ACTION: Is the no 2 element of planning is the necessary steps, tasks that need to be taken before a goal can be accomplished.
- IMPLEMENTATION: Is the no 3 element. This part is very important in the 4 key element of planning is the step/ process and

execution of plans in order to achieve a common goal.

- RESOURCES: Is the last key elements of planning. It is all about financing the plans i.e. by cash, property, asset and much more to make the dream of a business or an individual comes to reality.

Guide against being defrauded online by scams

This Term scam is so annoying and frustrating.

Frustrating or not, we don't have a choice than to prevent ourselves from falling a victim to scam/ cybercrime personal i.e. By not disclosing our secret to anyone, More so by not giving anyhow person access to our vital information to avoid falling victim of a scam.

These are The 10 Things To do to avoid being scam

Sign up for scam alerts from the government. To get the latest insight and advice about scams trying to send a message to you via email

Always hang up on robocalls . Whenever you noticed a recorded sales pitch while receiving a call hang up and report to the police because such calls are illegal, and the product are always bogus. Ensure you did not press 1 to speak to someone or to be taken away from the list. That may lead to more calls.

Avoid Spot imposters i.e. Scams are always pretending to be trusted, like government bodies, a charity, a family member or a firm you do Business with. Avoid sending money and vital information in response to a sudden request perhaps it comes as a text, an email or a phone call.

Always do online searches i.e. a product name, a company into a search engine like Google with world like scam, review and much more.

Stop Believing your caller <ID> Technology has made it easy for scams to cook up a false story i.e. If anyone calls and asking you for money or unnecessary demands. Hang up and report the case right away.

Avoid paying upfront for a promise. People might ask you pay in advance for things like loan offers, debts relief and much more. They might say you have a price to be claimed , but you must pay some money for you to get the gift.

Be careful on how you pay. Cards like credit card have significant fraud protections that are in built. Also take note wiring of money through Money gram, western union are very delicate because you may not recover your money back anymore. Always to talk someone. Seek advice from people before giving out your personal information or money out to someone you just meet that is demanding for it. Be extraordinary careful about free offers. These are strategies used by scams to operate and steal people vital information and used it against them Do not deposit a cheque or a wire money back it is very risky and much more.

Work Towards your goal

Working towards one goal is very important and must be taken serious Their is an adage that says It is Better to do some work well while young than to spend all the time in play i.e. Because any minute gone can never be regain Because time is money.

For a goal to be achievable we need to first know what we want because without it no goal can be set or achievable. Their is a term called <SMART>
S stands for specific
M stands for measurable
A stands for Attainable
R stands for Relevant
T stands for Time Bound
Think of a goal that motivates you take note of it to enable it as a tangible asset afterwards have a plan towards the goal that has been codified in a single document. And start executing it as fast as you can because later can become never.

Why do you need to set a goal?

you need to set up a goal because successful business people today and achievers in all ramifications ones set up a goal and they work towards it during the time of pain, awkward moment but they devoted their time and they made a lot of sacrifices that is why they later become successful today. You hear Forbes mentioning names of great people today and their impacts in the society. Without a goal and plan they cannot achieve that. I Challenge you today to work towards your goals and do not abandon it because of difficulties you are facing in it. Know this after any difficulties their is always a relief i.e. No pain no gain besides no shortcut to success if you want to be an overnight successful person you must be an everyday hustler that is the fact you must know. <u>Vast Tips for setting your Goals are as follows</u>

The listed Information above will help you and guide you to set achievable goals.

- Enumerate each goal as a positive statement: Say your goals positively by following these techniques and strategy it would enable your goal come true and avoid making any silly mistakes it is very important.

- Be specific about your goal: Set specific goals, by putting in times, dates and amounts by by doing this it would enable you to measure your achievement. If you can do this, you will be aware when you have achieved the goal without anybody reminding you of that, you will definitely be satisfied by achieving the goals.

- You must set priorities: When you have a lot of goals, give each goal a priority. This would enable you feeling overwhelmed by having so many goals, It will help you direct your attention to the important ones.
- Document your goals: This enables you to know the ones that has been executed and the pending ones.
- Always keep operational goals small: Ensure you keep the lower goals that you are working towards small and make it achievable through your efforts. If a goal is too big , It may seem you are not making progress towards it. Keeping goal lower and incremental gives more opportunities for incentives.
- You must set performance goals not the outcome goals: Ensure you take care to set goals over the time which you have much

control as possible. It may be tedious to achieve a personal goal for reasons beyond our capacity.

In the business world, the reasons could be constraint of bad business area or unplanned government policy. i.e. Sports, may include bad weather, injury, poor judging and much more.
NOTE: If you base your goal s on personal performance, you can as well control over the achievement of your goals, and get satisfaction from them.

- You must set realistic goals: It is essential to set a targeted goal that can be achievable. They are a lot of people i.e. parents, employers, society or media may set unachievable goals for you. They will always do this in negligence of your own desires and ambitions .

It is possible to set goals that are complicated because you might not see to the obstacles in the way, or get the clearer picture of how much skill you would need to develop and achieve a particular level of performance.

ACHIEVEMENT OF GOALS

When a goal has been achieved, you need to take the time to enjoy the satisfaction of taking the bold step to make it happen. You must Absorb the implications of the goal i.e. achievement and watch the progress that you have made towards other target/goals. By having the experience of achievement. Use the same strategy to implement your other goals.

- If you observed a deficit in your skills despite achieving the goal, decide whether you can set goals to fix it.
- If your goal took a dispiriting length of period to achieve, make the next goal easy
- If you have the opportunity to learn something that would lead you to change other goals, please do.

- If your goal is achieved with ease make your next goal rigid.

The lessons you have learned in this passive income Book into the methodology of setting your next goals.
Have it at the back of your mind that your goals will definitely change as time goes on. Always adjust them regularly to appear development in your knowledge and experience, and if goals does not have any attraction anymore, you have to consider them irrelevant and letting them goal would be the next option.

ILLUSTRATION OF PERSONAL GOALS

For his New Year Resolution, John has made a bold step to think about what he really wants to achieve with his life.

His lifetime goals are listed below:

- Physical: To run marathon very fast

- Career: To be in charge of managing editor of magazine I earn a living
- Artistic: To be copying my skills. Because I want to have my own display in the downtown gallery.

Now that we are aware about john has listed his lifetime goals, he now break down his lifetime career goal: By becoming managing editor of his magazine.

- His five –year goal: He want to Become a deputy editor
- One year goal: He decided to volunteer for projects that the current Managing Editor is coming up.
- A month goal: To be able to talk to the current managing editor to determine the skills needed to do the job.
- A week goal: To organise a meeting with the managing director.

As you can see clearly from the illustration below, he break big goals down into smaller i.e. more manageable goals makes it far easier to see how the goals can be achievable.

<u>VALUABLE KEY POINTS</u>

Goal setting is an important method for the followings:

- By deciding what you want to achieve in your life
- Self motivation
- Having self confidence: About successful Achievement of goals.
- Ensuring that their is separation between what's important and what is irrelevant.

If you do not have goals, do so now, Action is very important.

Make sure you make this methodology part of your life, you will definitely find your career improving, and you will be amazed how you did without these principles.

HOW TO EARN MONEY LEGITIMATELY ONLINE

Now we will be analyzing and explaining the different ways to make passive income online legitimately from your homes.

This area is very important for us to learn new skills that can put food on our table anytime. They are as follows:

- Being a computer literate: This is one of the most important skills that are generally useful worldwide and anybody reading this Book must make sure he or she learns the skills. It is very important and helpful in all ramifications of life.

Computer literacy is being knowledgeable and ability to operate computers & Technology properly. It is an important skill that anybody must have i.e. It makes life easy to live, it saves time and much more!

Computer literacy is a must have skill to possess. Entrepreneurs want their employees to have the necessary basic skills about computers; most companies are depending on computers to carry out their day to day activities. Besides when talking about communicating- computers are preferable than book and pen because information can be easily edited on computer.

Computer literacy is the skills and knowledge necessary for basic use of computer software, hardware and internet.

Computer skills are appreciated and valued in today's professional environments & Academic institutes.

It also lead to success in employment and education since computer skills are necessary to all area of studies

Educators are working hard to empower the public about the knowledge of computer.

Customer's services: Is the term that facilitate provision of services to prospect before, during and after a purchase has been made. The perception towards success of such conversation is dependent on the workers who are capable of adjusting themselves to the level of the visitor.

Customer service entails the priority of the firm assigned to the client to customer service related to component such as pricing and production innovation. In a nutshell a firm that appreciates good client services can spend more funds in seminars i.e. Training of their workers beyond average organization that can as well interview clients for feedback.

From the perspective of review of an overall return in sales i.e. By converting engineering effort, customer service plays a vital role in any organizations capability to generate income and revenue. From that reasoning customer service should be included as part of an approach of methodology improvement. A good perception of a clients can change the reasoning faculty of the prospect towards the organization.

- ## <u>Generating income from fever</u> : If you have a digital skills to offer to the world i.e. writing skills, graphic designs, networking make money on fever will be easy for you that is why it is important to learn new skills that are listed in this passive income Book for you to earn a good living. If you are good enough about your skill and you deliver what you promise to a high standard and within the schedule period of time frame. You can use the opportunity to make money because fever it is a platform for professionals to showcase their skills and make more money online

Here are 15 ways to make good money on fiverr

Through designing of flyers: If you are a graphic designer fiverr is for you no two ways about it.

Through Taking pictures with signs: By making a good picture of you holding up a sign standing close to a landmark in your vicinity you should be rest assured of daily income.

Through Designing of Business card: organizations are always in need of business card if you are good at designing business cards you will make money from fiverr.

Through Alter pictures: If you can erase the background off a picture by using Photoshop. You can make money on fiverr

Through virtual assistant: you can make a good cash if you can be doing a virtual assistant for a few hours daily.

Through Research: You can make a good cash by making use of the search engine called Google to explore for a project as long you are providing the right information to the prospect keep smiling to your Bank account.

Through creating digital drawings: If you are knowledgeable about how to use an automated photo-based drawing tools, you can design/create a digital drawing. People will pay you because they are always looking for custom graphics.

Through using marketing software to be paid: They are much sort of traffic generation software that you can use to promote prospect sites. If you can do this fiverr will get you daily money

Through fast writing & get paid: If you are a fast writer, you can get good cash from the channel.

Through offering social media services: If you can make use of social media to run a sponsor ad on facebook, instagram, Google. You can make money on the Blog

Through offering eBooks/ reports you have written: If you have this service and good enough to prove to the world you are better at it. you will always smile to your Bank account.

Fiverr is a platform that comprises of professional that are ready to showcase and launch their skills to the world.

As you are reading this book, I urge you to take advantage of feverr to make good money daily.

- Digital marketing skills: Is all about making your business visible online i.e. through having Business page across social media platforms such as Facebook, Instagram, Google my business, Twitter, Telegram and much more. You will also consider running sponsor ad on facebook, instagram and Google to sell your product fast online. Before you run a Facebook advert you must do research about your audience through Facebook audience insight tools with this it will enable to optimize your Facebook ad and instagram ad efficiently and wisely. You have to know the age range of people that need your product broad targeting is not good you need to target specific group of people that would be interested in your product. Their location is important too, you have to do research about where they spend most of their time only too.

You also need good graphic/ video to grab the attention of your customers online, you must also have a good content for them to be interested in the product you are showing to them. You must also have a good sales funnel i.e. a good website page for them to take a specific action on your website, so that you will not waste money on sponsor ad without getting a good result for your money. Also ensure you do retargeting advert for customers that have seen your product before but they are yet to purchase. It is very important so that they can later buy from you because if you don't retarget them they will later buy that same product from your competitors . You have to register yourself in your customer's mind .

If you can follow all these explanation below you will not have any problem with social media marketing and it will enable you to optimize your sponsor ad for you to get a better result from the money you invested in through sponsor ad.

- STOCK EXCHANGE: The word stock exchange is all about a means an investor is allow buying and selling shares of a company between each other in a regulated and legitimate space. You can as well go into this field and make more money by following the rules attached to it. I.e. an exchange can be described as a locale where things/asset is traded where manufacturer and customers meet for the purpose of buying and selling. More so financial product that can be traded includes commodities, derivatives, currencies and much more. Modern financial exchanges evolved from open outcry auctions literally on the streets of London or New York to highly regulated standard.

Now we would be looking at the purpose of a stock Exchange: When a firm/business raises capital through issuing shares, the owner of the new shares would be willing to sell their stake someday. Perhaps they have children going to school and need to pay up his outstanding in school. Maybe they now pass away, and their estate has been subjected to some hefty estate taxes. They might even leave it to their grandchildren, who get to enjoy the stepped-up basis loophole, and the heirs want to liquidate to purchase a house . Whatever prompt their decision, they are not likely to tie up their funds unless they are aware somehow, later in the future they will be able to find a buyer for their holdings without tedious efforts is the term called secondary market.

LIST OF BIG STOCK EXCHANGES IN THE WORLD

New York stock Exchange
Tokyo stock Exchange
NASDAQ
Shanghai stock Exchange
Euronext
Hong Kong stock Exchange

Shenzhen stock Exchange

London stock Exchange

TMX Group

Bombay stock Exchange

Deutsche Borse

National Stock Exchange of India

SIX Swiss Exchange

Korea Exchange

NASDAQ Nordic

Now we will be differentiating between a stock Exchange and a commodity market.

A stock exchange is a place where pieces of business owners stock are bought and sold among investors.

A commodity market exchange is described as where products/goods that are natural i.e. gold, silver, oil and much more are bought and sold among parties that is not for investment purposes but for the reason of usage in business operations.

- Travelling and Tours Agency: The term travelling and tour is a very lucrative business today because people love adventures i.e. they love to visit popular cities of the world with their family. Summer period & winter period. Some people preferred travelling summer period and some winter period. The love visiting city like New York city, Dubai, London, Dublin and much more. You use this opportunity to also venture into travelling agency and consultancy. The task is all about applying for a visa for clients, Booking of Tickets for clients, Hotel reservation, Taking the clients tour around the world. It is indeed a lucrative and easy job to do, provided you are knowledgeable about the internet and digital skills that is all you need to create passive income from this Travelling consultancy Business.

- VIDEO MAKING: Video production is the method of creating video content i.e. it is all about film making, more so with images recorded digitally instead of filming. This is also a Niche that will bring a good passive income when you are knowledgeable about the skills required to make a good videos for the prospect. It is an industry of actor and actress without video making they cannot make their money. This is also a Niche you can go into and you will worriless about money.

- **SELLING OF MUSICS:** This is one of the lucrative niches too. It is all about publishing music for sales online to big stores like Amazon, YouTube and much more

These are the steps to follow to sell music online:
You must Record a few songs
You must Have your music Available in multiple formats..
You can sell your music through digital apps and music stores...
You must join a digital distribution network
Sell your beats and Instrumental music online to get results faster.
You must sell physical copies of your music online
You can also sell your music in person
You can promote your music through social media

You should always perform at every opportunity or events.

You should send your music to radio stations

Hire an agent for your music

You should send your music to some record label

All the explanation below is to give you a guide on what to do this Book is about educating you to take advantage of the internet to make passive income legitimately from your end.

- **SELLING OF INFORMATION PRODUCTS:** Selling of information product is a very good niche to tap into.

Information product is all about selling online seminar training, publication of magazines, EBooks and much more. It is a niche that does not require much capital to start. It is all about having a good sales funnel for the information products. Information product as fetch a lot of young entrepreneur good money because they have the necessary skills to venture into the business.

The information provided in this Book would have given you Big money mindset by now and I urge to take massive actions. Moreso you have to know big money mindset is all about:

Making more money Everyday

You have to know that Business is a competition and it is not for the weak.

Money is a mindset & Action game

Money love speeds

Money makes you more of who you are.

ANALYSIS

All features of money listed below is to equip you to take massive actions and invest i.e. it does not matter how much you have at the moment the zeal in you is what matters and can make you achieved your goals only by risking the usual for the unusual also <NOTE> You either make money or make Excuses, but not both you never stop learning and acquiring new skills. Creativity is very essential in Business it makes you dynamic in nature and it also makes you standout in your niche. More so always listen to news everyday it will help you grow and it will help your Business grow.

CONCLUSION

I strongly believe this Book as provided the general public a good insight towards self development, job opportunities, Internet as a legitimate source of Income, Marketing principles and much more. With the analysis so far I strongly believe you can scale up and be successful in life.

The key is massive Actions, with massive Actions you will move from where you are to where you ought to be.
Stay blessed.
THIS BOOK END HERE.